Flat Belly for Life Revisited

Flat Belly for Life Revisited

A HOLISTIC GUIDE TO LIVING A HEALTHY, MEANINGFUL LIFE INTO YOUR 100'S

Mike McLeod

ISBN: 1973855283
ISBN 13: 9781973855286

Disclaimer

am not a doctor or medical professional. The information in this book is for the education of the reader. It is not medical advice and is not intended to cure any disease. You should consult with a doctor for professional medical advice. For licensed providers of TA 65, contact TA Sciences, and someone will call you. Also, you may check the website Revgentics.com.

Dedication

This book is dedicated to my late mother Frances McLeod. Despite the fact that she was a Type 1 diabetic who had to take insulin shots, she lived to be 95. This was despite the fact that she did not have the best of medical care at her home in rural South Georgia. She was a member of a family that grew up on a small farm in South Georgia. Her two brothers were veterans of the Normandy Invasion in World War II.

Neither of her brothers had any more than a high school education. However, both of them became successful local businessmen. In the words of NBC News anchor Tom Brokaw, they were part of "America's Greatest Generation". All of my mother's sisters except one married men far better off than my father. That one never married at all and became a school superintendent in Montgomery, Alabama. My mother had enough college education to teach school when she got married. Unfortunately, my father was an insecure little guy who did not help her get a car that was necessary to be a school teacher in rural Georgia.

I inherited from my mother not only the love of literature, but also the love of learning that enabled me to overcome the poverty that I was born into. Ever since I read Ernest Hemingway's classic little book "The Old Man and the Sea" I wanted to be an author. Mother subscribed to the Reader's Digest condensed book club. Every month we would receive in the mail a new volume of these condensed books—each containing 4 to 6 books. I still have several of these books in my library today. They are supplemented by the leather bound collection of the 100 Greatest Books of All Time published by the Franklin Library..

Acknowledgements and Author's Note

t is noted that this is an update from my original book published in 2016. Things have changed a lot in my personal life since I wrote my previous book.

All of the changes in my physical and mental condition have been positive. I can see the rapid growth of new skin, new nails and new hair. My skin looks as youthful as ever —no more age spots. I have the need to clip my nails at least twice a week. After dying my hair for years, I have stopped, and the brown roots have come out.

As for my mental condition, I have just taken up the hard intellectual challenge of trading options. This is my first book for 2017, but I plan to write at least one book for the next few years.

A few years ago medical science was not advanced enough to have enabled me to make the recommendations that are now in this book.

I wish to thank Dr. Michael Fossel MD, Ph.D., and the leading anti-aging doctor in the world. His latest book is "The Telomerase Revolution: The Enzyme That Holds the Key to human aging…and Will Soon Lead to Longer, Healthier Lives". This is not his first book. He has been writing similar books for over a decade, and his message has been consistent throughout. Fossel's current mission is to cure Alzheimer's disease. He is doing so through his company Telocyte.

In addition, Fossel has been kind enough to send autographed copies to his latest book to some of my old friends whose evidence of aging has worried me.

The other person I want to thank is Dr. Ed Park, the author of "Telomere Time bombs: Defusing the Terror of Aging". Without his book and series of podcasts I would never have known Dr. Fossel. Dr. Park was one of the first doctors to try out TA 65 on himself. He did so as a part of a select group of medical doctors. He does a good job of simplifying his message so that people other than medical professionals can understand it.

All of us owe a debt of gratitude to the three scientists who won the Nobel Prize in 2009 for their discovery of how chromosomes are protected by telomeres and the enzyme telomerase. They are Elizabeth H. Blackburn, Carol W. Greider, and Jack W. Szostak.

On a personal note, I want to thank the medical scientists who have pursued the cures for cancer. As I related in my previous book, "The Death of Civility and Common Sense", I lost two of my friends and heroes too early to cancer. The first was Senator and former Vice President Hubert Humphrey, who died of cancer in his mid-60s. The second was former Congressman and Secretary of Agriculture Ed Madigan, who died of lung cancer at the age of 52 when he was a member of my law firm.

Recently, former President Jimmy Carter, who is 92, was diagnosed as having cancer of the liver and the brain. However, after some treatment he was pronounced to be cancer-free. He was always fit and was known as a runner, even when he was President. President George H.W. Bush is 93. Either of these men could live to be 100, the first American President to do so. Bob Dole, another old friend who tried but failed to be President, is also 93. He is wheelchair bound, but his mind is as sharp as ever.

And last, I wish to thank Senator Herman Talmadge, who lived to be 88. Fortunately, he did not have cancer, His wife Lynda took good care of him until his death. With the medical advances in the last few years, I feel confident that Talmadge could have lived past 100. Without him I would never met Humphrey, Madigan, or Carter. Talmadge always had a flat belly because he was always was a runner and walker. I think I was inspired to run by his example. I remember him dictating a letter to his oldest son, urging him to walk more and lose weight. It reminded me of Lord Chesterfield's letters to his son. Unfortunately, his son did not heed his advice. He died at the relatively young age of 71.

Why I wrote this book

As I reached my 70's a number of my old friends began to die. First, I got a call from the wife of a friend of mine who had started his work as the chief counsel of the House Agriculture Committee at the same time that I started my career as chief counsel of the Senate Committee on Agriculture, Nutrition and Forestry. Both of us were 74. His wife told me he had passed away. This hit me hard. I had rented an office to him one door down from my own office in my law firm until he retired a few years ago.

Next, I traveled to Chicago to race in the "Hustle up the Hancock" race that is held every year the last weekend of February. It is a challenging race up 94 floors of the John Hancock building. While I did not win, I got a medal for competing. One of the race officials asked me why I was competing, I responded that this was the only way I could control my weight.

During my visit to Chicago, I visited by phone with one of my oldest personal and professional friends. Although he was not able to travel to downtown Chicago to visit with me, he sounded strong. His wife and he had been good friends of my wife and me for many years. I returned to Washington, DC, but was shocked a week later to hear he had died of a heart attack.

A very successful lawyer and lobbyist that I knew died at the age of 73. His skinny little mother lived to be 97. That is two decades of healthy living his pot belly could have cost him.

During the last two years, I have contacted several old friends to urge them to take TA 65. Some have suspected that I might have a financial interest in this supplement. **Let me be clear. I have no financial interest whatever in TA Sciences. My only interest is in not losing old friends.**

Preface

Although this book deals with physical fitness, mental fitness is just as important. As I was beginning this book, I visited the Torpedo Factory in Old Town, Alexandria, Virginia. This was an abandoned factory where torpedoes were manufactured in World War II. Marian Van Landingham was the volunteer community activist who would lead the effort to transform this old dump on the waterfront of Alexandria into an artist center.

It now houses an amazing assortment of local artists who stay busy creating and selling their wares. The Torpedo Factory is busy with the both locals and tourists, especially on the weekends. There are two thriving waterfront restaurants next to it and new condo buildings across the street. On weekends you cannot get seated in the restaurants without advance reservations.

I happened upon an old lady whose shop is on the top floor. She is several years older than I. She was busy producing a new painting when I came upon her late on a Saturday afternoon. I recognized that she was Marian Van Landingham. When I introduced myself, she did not seem old at all. She was doing something she loved, and it was not work to her.

The lesson in this is that mental activity is just as important as physical activity in halting aging. People need a purpose in life to get out of bed each morning after they are past retirement age. It can be painting, writing, community service or other things they enjoy. They are life time learners.

In my own case, I am learning to trade options in my modest stock portfolio. It is the hardest thing I have ever tried to learn, but boy, does it exercise my brain! I try to devote some time every day to this. I have be scammed out of some money in this effort, but it has been a learning process.

Life is not a destination. It is a journey.

There are thousands of diet and exercise books out there, and you probably don't need to hear my life story. I will cut to the chase. Let's look at the time line of some remarkable scientific achievements:

In recent years there have been several books on ending aging, reversing aging, or curing aging. Just about all of them miss the mark. I have read most of them. Every summer there is a big meeting of the coalition for radical life extension (RADs) where hundreds of people gather to hear distinguished speakers. It appears many of them are more interested in the industry of curing aging <u>than actually doing something about aging</u>. Fortunately, I heard about the discovery of TA 65 over three years ago. This substance is already curing or reversing aging.

Below is the recent timeline —-beginning in 1961--for this scientific achievement. For a longer timeline, see Dr. Fossel's 2015 book "The Telomerase Revolution: The Enzyme That Holds the Key to Human Aging… and Will Soon Lead to Longer, Healthier Lives". His book goes further back into medical history—beginning in 1665.

1961

American anatomist Leonard Hayflick put forward the theory that our cells will only divide a limited number of times. He demonstrated that a population of normal human fetal cells in a cell culture will divide only between 40 to 60 times. When our cells cease to divide, we die. This natural phenomena is known as the "Hayflick Limit". Incidentally, I understand that Hayflick is alive and well at the age of 88.

1971

Russian scientist Alexey Olnikov published his thesis that the shortening of telomeres is the mechanism responsible for the Hayflick Limit.

1982

Elizabeth Blackburn discovered that telomeres have a particular DNA.

1990

Michael West founded the Geron Corporation with the goal of finding a way to intervene in the aging process based on telomere research.

1992

Calvin Harley and his colleagues at the Geron Corporation discovered that children with Hutchinson-Gilford progeria disease are born with short telomeres. This causes these children to die of "old age" by the age of 13.

1993

Based on Geron's research, Michael Fossel began work on the first book about understanding how and why aging occurs. "Reversing Human Aging" was published in 1996. Also, Fossel has authored the first and only medical textbook on this subject.

1997-1998

Michael Fossel authored the first peer-reviewed articles in the Journal of the American Medical Association that suggested that telomerase might be used to treat age-related diseases.

1999

The Geron Corporation demonstrated that telomere shortening is not only related to cell aging but causes it, and that re-lengthening telomeres resets the aging in cells.

2000

The Geron Corporation patented the use of astragalosides for the use of telomerase activators.

2002

Geron and other research laboratories demonstrated that the lengthening of telomeres reverses aging, not only in cells but in human tissues as well,
    Also, in 2002 the Geron Corporation shelved pharmaceutical development of telomerase activators to concentrate on cancer therapies. Geron then sold the nutraceutical rights for astragalosides to Noel Thomas Patton. He established a new company called TA Sciences in New York City

2003

Sierra Sciences was founded by Bill Andrews, who was at the Geron Corporation when TA 65 was discovered. Since he founded Sierra Sciences it has been conducting research on screening potential telomerase activation products. It continues this research and sells a product called Product B. This product does not rely on the molecule extracted from the Astragalus root that is the basis of TA 65. Sierra Sciences continues research and the improvement of its products today. I am told by the company officials that it is not wise to buy this product from third party sellers.

2004

The Oxford University Press published the textbook "Cells, Aging, and Human Disease" by Michael Fossel.

2006

TA Sciences marketed the first nutraceutical telomerase activator, TA 65. It was derived from the plant Astragalus membranaceus

2007

After five years of development and safety testing, the first capsules were administered to a small group of anti-aging doctors. One of these was Dr. Ed Park, who has become the leading popularizer of TA 65.

2009

Together with Jack Szostak, Elizabeth Blackburn further proved that this DNA prevents chromosomes from being broken down. Blackburn, Carol Greider, and Jack Szostak won the Nobel Prize for the discovery of the enzyme telomerase, which produces the telomeres' DNA.

2010

A different kind of book was published. It was written by Michael Fossel MD, PHD, Greta Blackburn, and Dr. Dave Woynarowski MD. Its title is "The Immortality Edge". It gave a very balanced picture of advances in progress toward extending human lives, but the most significant was the discovery of TA 65.

2011

The Geron Corporation sold the rights to all their telomerase activators to TA Sciences.

June 2016

Until this date, there was no clinical proof that TA 65 worked in humans. However, in June 2016 the first randomized, double blind and placebo controlled test was published. It is published in the press release issued by TA Sciences that is reproduced later in this book.

Bill Andrews' Contributions

Andrews is also a good resource for the timeline for curing aging. You may refer to his website www.sierrasci.com for the latest scientific advances. The company continues to do research and sells his Product B. I have recently started taking this, with favorable results, especially in better sleep.

What strikes me is the accelerating speed of this timeline in the last ten years

For those who have the interest and time to read this nine hour book I highly recommend the book "Happy Accidents: Serendipity in Major Medical Breakthroughs in the Twentieth Century" by Morton A. Myers, M.D. . Some of the examples are antibiotics, Viagra and cancer drugs.

We are now well into the twenty first century but the parallels are impressive. TA 65 was discovered quite by accident as the Geron Corporation pursued a cure for cancer. When the corporation discovered what is called TA 65 instead, it sold the patents to Noel Thomas Patton. This was obviously based of their economic analysis that there would be far more money to be made in developing a drug to cure cancer.

As Winston Churchill once said, ''Men occasionally stumble upon the truth, but most pick themselves up and hurry off as if nothing happened''.

The history of fitness - Charles Atlas

The first great body builder was Charles Atlas. He was born Angelo Siciliano in 1892 and was the developer of a bodybuilding method and accompanying exercise. It was cleverly promoted by an advertising campaign. He legally changed his name to Charles Atlas when a friend told him that he looked like the statute of Atlas on a hotel on Coney Island,

Even my oldest brother, who grew up on a farm working hard in the fields every day bought his mail order courses. This was because Atlas promised to help you build a great body using dynamic tension.

Dynamic Tension is a self-resistance exercise method which pits muscle against muscle. The practitioner tenses the muscles of a given body part and then moves the body part against the tension as if a heavy weight were being lifted. Dynamic Tension exercises are not merely isometrics, since they call for movement. Instead, the method comprises a combination of exercises in three disciplines: isotonic, isokinetic, and some exercises in the isometric discipline.

Proponents asserted that it is nearly impossible to be injured doing these exercises because one's own muscles provide the force and, as they tire, so the force used also decreases. Likewise, the benefits can continue beyond the more traditional exercise methods because as the practitioner grows stronger, the exercise becomes more intense.

Also, dynamic tension requires no special equipment or gym memberships, so it was affordable for all income groups. Although Charles Atlas died in 1972, the course is still available on the website, www. charlesatlas.com.

The Godfather of Modern Fitness--Jack LaLanne

Another example is Jack LaLanne. He had no bulky muscles, but was stronger than Arnold Schwarzenegger. When a 21-year-old Schwarzenegger first came to America in 1968, he witnessed 54-year-old Jack LaLannne down on Venice Beach in California doing thousands of push-ups and chin-ups. A challenge was declared — and Arnold, the youngest Mr. Universe at the time, went on to lose badly.

"I beat him in chin-ups and push-ups," LaLanne said. Arnold then said, 'That Jack LaLanne's an animal! I was sore for four days. I couldn't lift my arms."

I also heard that years later he invited some fitness guru to come and attempt one of his legendary challenges filled with push-ups, chin-ups, and a host of other high-intensity workouts. LaLanne crushed him — even in his late 80s.

As a small boy, I saw LaLanne going through his prodigious exercise routines on daytime television. That was my first real introduction to modern physical fitness.

He had an attitude described as fierce, but even Jack would tell it straight if asked. When questioned whether age ever got in the way of his goals, LaLanne once said:

"I train like I'm training for the Olympics or for a Mr. America contest (a title which he once held), the way I've always trained my whole life. You see, life is a battlefield. Life is survival of the fittest. How many healthy people do you know? Think about it. People work at dying, they don't work at living. My workout is my obligation to life. It's my tranquilizer. It's part of the way I tell the truth — and telling the truth is what's kept me going all these years." His slogan was "The rest of your life is the best of your life".

Jack LaLanne was known as "the godfather of fitness", and was considered a crackpot when he was younger. He was a good 50 years ahead of his time. He opened the first modern gym in 1936 even though the doctors were against him. They said working out with weights would give people heart attacks, and that a man would lose his sex drive and women would look like a man. Even the coaches and athletes were afraid they would get musclebound.

At the age of 95, Jack completed his book, "Live Young Forever: 12 Steps to Optimum Health, Fitness & Longevity". There is a photo of him doing a handstand at 95. His slogan was "the rest of your life is the best of your life". It is a good book to read, but it is now available only as a used book on Amazon.com.

LaLanne lived to the age of 96. With today's advances in anti-aging medicine, he surely would have lived to be well over 100.

My personal fitness journey

My own flat belly is due to two things-- diet and (HIIT). This means high intensity interval training.

I have been running and jogging all of my adult life. I started when I was in basic training for the Army National Guard. This happened after I graduated from law school and went into the Army for my boot camp training at Fort Leonard Wood, Missouri.

I was a very out-of-shape recruit. As a member of the Capitol Police Force I had been at a desk at one of the entrances to the US Capitol Building. As a part of the midnight shift, I worked from midnight until dawn and went to law school during the day and the early evening. Obviously, my sleep pattern was poor.

I barely passed the physical examination for the Army because I had fallen arches, a condition that would plague me later in life when I was over the age of 60. I now realize that this was because I was too fat. I weighed 195 pounds when I had my physical examination. Moreover, I did not have a rich father to pay a doctor to write an opinion that I was unfit for service.

During my basic training at the boot camp in Fort Leonard Wood, Missouri the drill sergeants made us run all the time. I remember that one old fat boy collapsed by the side of the road and a burly drill sergeant hit him with a rifle butt and made him get up. This was during the height of the War in Vietnam and we were being prepared to go directly into combat. One of our exercises was to crawl through the mud at night under live fire. We also practiced throwing live grenades and fighting with bayonets

We trainees were so tired that we would fall asleep when we sat down on the ground with our backs against a tree. When we had a meal in the mess halls, the drill sergeants would walk around yelling at us "eat up and get out you sons of bitches". I had always been a slow eater, but I learned to quickly devour my food. It took me decades to get out of this habit.

An old friend in Congress from North Carolina never did overcome this habit, and he died at the young age of 73.

The lungs of many trainees were not in any condition to take this extreme exercise, so the coughing at night in our barracks made it sound like a tuberculosis ward.

When I began basic training I weighed 195 pounds. When I completed basic training, I weighed only 145 pounds--a loss of 50 pounds.

Ever since the army, I have been trying to replicate that experience. I have tried running and jogging. It helped, but nothing seemed to work completely. With every passing year the pounds creeped back on. My wife would point out that I was getting a pot belly. I wound resent it. When my son was just a toddler, I put him in a baby carriage with bicycle wheels on the rear so that I could run around the neighborhood with him strapped in. I am sure this was a strange sight for the neighbors.

Only recently did I discover high intensity interval training or HIIT. This involves strenuous training with short bursts of activity. For me the best way to do this is stair climbing or hill climbing. I do both. You can also try running on a treadmill or stair climbing machine. I have both at home. Although I have tried them, they never worked for me. A bonus for me is that when I finish my runs the first thing every morning I shower using a Japanese exfoliating body scrub. I then feel better than I have ever felt in my life.

I should add that I fell for my share of fitness scams along the way. One was a vibrating machine supposedly used by the astronauts and some injured football players. They can be purchased at many online sites and even at Walmart. These machines may have been useful for astronauts in a gravity free atmosphere but they are worthless for healthy people on planet earth. I bought one for my apartment in the Washington area. Eventually, I just took it to the trash.

Diet

Your diet should be a combination meat and fish complimented by fresh vegetables and fruit.

There are many books on paleo diets. They were all the rage a few years ago. However, the paleo diet has not worked for some people. That's because some people find it impossible to stay on this diet.

A good general rule is that about 35 percent of calories consumed should be meat or fish. It makes a large difference where your other calories come from. They should come as much as possible from fresh fruits and vegetables. This means the kind of food our ancestors ate-- meat, fish, and raw fruits and vegetables. A strict paleo diet excludes grains and dairy products. I take exception to this. My usual breakfast is a little bowl of blueberries or other fruit in milk with a few scoops of whole grain cereal. At my other meals, I may have a small serving of whole wheat bread. After dinner, I often have an ice cream cone.

It is easy and convenient to consume protein drinks between meals. This helps you avoid unhealthy snacks. There are many convenient protein drinks available, such as the Atkins products. The Atkins drinks have 15 grams of protein. Other products, such as Premier Protein, have 30 grams of proteins. Another good snack is cubes of cheddar cheese, which has few carbohydrates.

Exercise

Aerobic exercise should be high intensity, such as stair running and mountain running. Some kind of weight lifting should be done to maintain muscle mass and strength. As a complement to your running, I recommend at least a dozen repetitions with dumb bells. Many trainers recommend planking exercises. With these, you lay down with your body in a rigid position with your body supported only by your elbows and toes. You maintain that position as long as you can. This strengthens your core.

I prefer to use small dumb bells while standing on a bosu ball. Avoid heavy weights. You need functional fitness--not big muscles to show off at the beach. Another handy tool is the Grip Master. I have one at my desk and try to use it twice a day. Evidence shows that today's men tend not have grips as strong as their fathers did because they have desk jobs working on computers. Men's grip strength tends to decline faster than that of women.. It also strengthens your forearms as well as assuring you never have a wimpy handshake.

My Stair Running Career

I had engaged in stair running for a few years and had run up the stairs of an office tower in Greenville, SC at the age of 74. Then I trained very hard and competed in the annual race up the 94 floors of the John Hancock building in Chicago, Illinois. I won a medal, but I was disappointed that I didn't finish first in the over-70 category. One of the race officials asked why I competed, and I responded that stair running was the only way I could lose weight. After I was through with the race, I retired from competition. I will try it again when I am over 80, just to see if I can win.

Since that race, I noticed that my weight increased by 10 pounds. Then I had an epiphany!! The reason I gained so much weight so quickly was that I was no longer using the high intensity running when I ran up the stairs. I had timed myself on my iWatch to see if I would be competitive. After checking this daily, I thought I would be competitive.

I finally concluded that a leisurely run up the stairs does not work. What is needed is a period of at least 30 seconds of high-intensity running followed by a period at least twice that long for slower exercise that allows you to catch your breath. I have since followed that principle, and I've noticed the pounds slowly came off again.

You have no need to time yourself. Just run until you are entirely winded. Stop and then run more stairs until you are entirely winded again.

Not everyone has to engage in stair running. It is one of the most distasteful exercises I have ever done. I try to do it only the first thing every morning. The main advantage is that after I finished, I feel better than I have ever felt in my life. It reminds me of the story about the little idiot who would hit himself on the head with a hammer because it felt so good when he stopped.

When I am at home in Asheville, NC I do enjoy running the mountain trails with my dog Zeus. I now realize that I must apply the HIIT principles. In running up the steep hills I need to be very intense until I am winded and then slow down long enough to catch my breath. I get my whole body into it by pumping my arms. Also I run on the balls of my feet and my toes to achieve this intensity. If I cannot feel my toes on the soles of my shoes, I know I am not being as intense as I should. Thus I consciously think "ball and toes". Then I slow down until I catch my breath and repeat the intense cycle.

I no longer worry about my distance or time spent running. I just try to get in at least 12 segments of high intensity running up hills. However, when you include the distances back down the hills as well as the steps taken throughout the day, it is about 3 miles.

On the equally long distances back down the mountains, I don't even try to get my pulse up. I have learned to be careful to avoid a bad fall. I know this to be a fact, because I once had a horrible fall.

I was walking and running two German shepherd dogs. The one that belonged to my son was an untrained dog with vicious tendencies. Then a neighbor lady walked her little dog up our driveway. Both dogs bolted for it. Because I had the leashes of two large dogs wrapped around my hands, they pulled me down. I hit my head on a large rock and the dogs dragged my face through the gravel and busted out my teeth.

I would have bled to death if my mountain resort staff had not been close by to call an ambulance and rush me to a nearby hospital. Even then, I was out cold for several hours and had to undergo a tough recovery period. Fortunately, a young woman who was the resident plastic surgeon came in and sewed up my face. All of this occurred on July 6, 2012, a day I shall never forget.

I insisted on getting back to work in a few days, but my wife objected, and insisted on coming with me. I had a client named Bob Haney who was flying into town to have lunch. When he came in, he took one look at me and said, "You shouldn't be here".

As a result of this traumatic near death experience, I have a new appreciation for living a healthy long life. I am now more determined than ever before to have a healthy life until I am in my 100's.

You can use a number of indoor exercises in lieu of outdoor exercises. The trick is to have a short period of high intensity training followed by period twice that long of slower exercise. Many people prefer spinning, or riding a stationary bike. The trick is to work out so long that you have to stop to catch your breath.

I have never been a good swimmer, so this is not an exercise that works for me. However there are others, like my wife, who prefers it. She worked as a lifeguard while growing up and is a good swimmer. One of its main benefits is that it is easy on your joints. I have noticed that my old friends who were long distance runners have had to stop because it wore out their joints. The exception that proves the rule is one friend who has never weighed over 120 pounds. He has competed in the Boston Marathon. He is in his early 70's and still running.

How to cure snoring through proper food and exercise

Snoring can cause problems in a marriage. Snoring is nothing but labored breathing. You should build up your lungs through HIIT exercises. Obviously, obese people snore more than others. When I was a small boy, an obese aunt would come to visit us and I could hear her snoring though the walls.

Later, my wife would complain about my snoring, and even had me tested for sleep apnea once. Now that I am in shape, she never complains any more. In fact, I now tell her that she snores more than I do. DISLAIMER--I did not say that she is fat or old!! You should never tell your wife that she is either of these things.

You should only sweeten your beverages with raw, unfiltered honey. Also, if you use sugar or sugar substitutes for other purposes, substitute honey. The old guy who taught me this said to use raw local honey, but I later found that it makes no difference whether it is local. However, I would draw the line if were imported from a foreign country. There is no longer any need to use a netti pot, saline rinse, strips on your nose or other device that is sold.

On the TV, you often see a guy selling his brand of pillow from his web site, www.mypillow.com. I think these are good because they encourage you to sleep on your side.

Brisk Walking is the next best thing to running

Next to running, fast walking is the best thing. I would shoot for 2 miles a day running and walking while working at my full time .job

When going through the huge Atlanta Airport I try to walk rather than ride the subway. I walk up the huge escalators if I can pass others. You should keep in mind that it must be brisk walking. My frequent airplane trips serve as a reminder of this. When the planes land and we get up to disembark, I notice that my legs are stiff, and I don't walk as fast as younger people.

I am convinced that my late mother lived to be 95 despite being a diabetic because she walked a lot. She lived almost all of her life in a small rural community. Because she had no automobile to drive, she walked to visit with family and friends. She also had to walk a lot to do her chores in raising three boys as well as tending her gardens. I am guessing that she averaged 2 to three miles of walking a day.

Lessons from History

As an ardent student of history, I noticed that John Adams, our second President, lived to be 90 years of age. Given the level of medical care at the time, that is remarkable. However, Adams was a farmer as well as country lawyer. Unlike George Washington before him and Thomas Jefferson after him, he did not have slaves to plough his fields. That meant that he had to walk behind mules to plough his fields.

Both Washington, who lived to be 67, and Jefferson, who lived to be 83, were vigorous outdoorsmen and horsemen. However, they did not have to walk a lot.

Much later Harry Truman was our President. He had been a farmer in his early years, but most farmers had tractors by then, so it was not necessary for him to plough a mule. When Truman became President he was known for taking brisk walks outside of the White House grounds every morning. To the consternation of his Secret Service detail, he became known as "the incredible walking President". Truman lived to be 88.

Standing up While Working is the Next Best Thing to Walking

In our white collar society too many people sit all day at the office and then come home and spend several hours on a couch watching the TV. The stand-up desk is the answer. Some of the younger lawyers in my law office worked from stand up desks. I recently followed suit and joined them--alternating between sitting down and standing up.

The Latest Gadgets are a Big Help

I was an early adopter of the iPhone. More recently, I was one of the first adopters of the iWatch. The iPhone and the iPad are perfect at giving your blood pressure readings. The iWatch is perfect for reading your heart rate. The iWatch will remind you to stand up and move around for one minute until you have done it for 12 times each day.

For over 40 years I struggled to keep my blood pressure within a permissible range. When I would have my annual physical, my doctor would caution that I was borderline hypertension. My systolic was slightly above 140 and my diastolic was slightly above 90. These numbers caused me to pay higher life insurance premiums for years. My doctor would caution me to reduce my salt intake and lose weight. Looking at some of my old photos, I can agree with his counsel to lose weight.

Now, my blood pressure is better than good. My diastolic is less than 60 and my systolic is less than 130. When I am at rest it is even lower.

Another heart number was my heart rate. To get your maximum heart rate, subtract your age from 220. Multiply that number by 0.7 (70 percent) to determine the lower end of your target heart rate zone. Then multiply your maximum heart rate by 0.85 (85 percent) to determine the upper end of your target heart rate zone.

In this case, I did better. Before a stair run I would strap on a Timex band with the sensor over my heart. At age 74, my heart rate would be a little over 120 when I completed my run up to the top of the stairs.

Get a good night's sleep

I have struggled with mild insomnia for years, and I read several books on insomnia. I have found that I function best on at least 7 hours a night. Nice deep sleep is necessary for our body cells to regenerate themselves. It enables our bodies to naturally produce Human Growth Hormone.

I sleep better when I run. A period of two minutes meditation before bed also helps. I have tried a number of medications, including massive doses of melatonin. However, what works best for me is a little sleep aids pill which has 50 milligrams of Diphenhydramine (HCL)" and another pill that has 500 mg of L-Tryptophan. Both of these are available for a minimal cost at amazon.com.

I am taking Product B sold by Sierra Sciences, the company of my friend Bill Andrews . It has caused me to seep better than I ever have. If this continues, I will no longer take the two items described above.

Cure Type 2 Diabetes. Use it as an excuse to have a healthy diet.

The only malady I now have is one I struggled with for several years. It is Type 2 Diabetes. Both of my parents had diabetes and had to take insulin in their later years. I never had to do that, but I was unable to enjoy pizza for several years because it is so high in carbohydrates. I tried hard to stick to a low carb diet, and that helped me lose weight.

I would stick my fingers with one of those little needles every day to test my blood sugar. However my combination of exercise and my daily dosage of TA and Metformin enabled me to get it under control.

However, it was not as good control as I thought. During my annual physical, my doctor noticed a spike in my blood sugar when he did a test. He prescribed a stronger and more expensive drug named Jardiance, which is working. The only other prescription or nonprescription medication I now take is two metformin tablets a day, a generic drug that costs 10 cents a tablet and another drug named Atorvastatin to ensure my arteries are clear.

Avail yourself of the abundant free advice on the Internet.

With the abundant free advice on many websites, there is no need to pay for a lot of medical advice. My favorites are: WebMD, Mayo Clinic House Call, Share Care, and the inimitable Dr. Oz. He was the author who inspired me to pursue a longer life in the book he authored with Dr. Roizen ten years ago. It is, "You, Staying Young: The Owner's Manual for Extending Your Warranty". Since then, he has authored several other books. He is a favorite of day time television, and a video of his shows can be automatically sent to you without charge.

Do not take the steroid human growth hormone (HGH) or even injections of testosterone.

Avoid expensive scams like those promoting human growth hormone (HGH), I once went to see a Cenergenics doctor who does prescribe it. These doctors advertise a lot on the financial channels on TV, the channels watched most by old men.

You don't need to build bulky muscles when you are over 50. You certainly don't need to inject yourself daily with illegal drugs. It cost me $2,000 a month and the doctor objected that I emailed him "more than any other patient did". It was also a multi-level marketing scheme because he gave me a 10% discount for people I referred to him. Regrettably, I referred my best friend in the Washington DC area to him. I fell for this scheme only because my dentist of over 35 years recommended him to me.

This doctor urged me to work out with heavy weights. I did so by going down to the gym in my apartment building every morning. I would look over at the other guys working out with those weights, and I was delighted if I saw that I was lifting larger weights or doing more reps than a younger guy.

The doctor did give me one helpful tip. He urged me to do stair running. He said I should go up the stairs as fast as possible, with my arms pumping

Then I found out that 13 people, including 5 doctors, 1 chiropractor, and 1 pharmacist, in Florida were indicted for selling human growth hormone (HGH). It was the Treasure Coast Pharmacy Scandal. It took place on September 1, 2011. You can google and find the Department of Justice press release of that date.

However, I found out about it only because my Cenergenics doctor complained that he had to find another source of his steroid supply. I then did the research that I should have done in the beginning. I accused this old doctor of malpractice and never took this stuff again. HGH should be outlawed for everyone except for those with special needs. Aging is not a special need. A good exercise regimen will cause your body to make all of the HGH you need.

One American, Tour de France winning biker Lance Armstrong, was caught taking steroids in 2013. He had been suspected for years. Armstrong had been an American hero because he had survived cancer and come back to be a champion again. He sold wrist bands to raise money for the American Cancer Society. When this doping was proved, he was stripped of his medals, and his career ended in disgrace. He had the HGC given to him by his trainer. Later a personal fitness trainer friend of mine in Asheville lost her boyfriend who was a bicycle racing trainer. He committed suicide.

See this description of HGH in WebMD:

"Synthetic human growth hormone was developed in 1985 and approved by the FDA for specific uses in children and adults. In children, HGH injections are approved for treating short stature of unknown cause as well as poor growth due to a number of medical causes, including: Turner's syndrome and other disorders."

I did go briefly to an anti-aging doctor in Asheville who prescribed injections of testosterone, which is safe. He never tried to prescribe HGH. I later heard about a cream from an old cab driver friend from Harlem named Fred Bell, who is my age. He said you can get the same benefits from a cream. Today I get DHEA cream from amazon.com for $25 and it lasts for several months. I changed apartments in Arlington, VA a couple of years ago, and I was aghast at the number of needles and syringes that I threw away.

Don't fall for Expensive and Unnecessary Supplements or Prescription Drugs

Ignore most of the claims of the $37 billion a year supplement industry. However it is not nearly bad as the pharmaceutical industry, which is estimated to be a $300 billion a year industry.

You can tell what a rich industry the pharmaceutical industry has become by the endless number of commercials they have on TV. Also, they have long disclaimers to protect themselves from the class action lawsuit industry. You are warned to take their drugs only under the supervision of your doctors, and advised that if there are any harmful side effects, the drug company is not responsible.

In 2016 there was a furor in Congress about Mylan, a large drug company, has jacked up the price of EpiPen, which is necessary to counter the allergic reaction known as anaphylaxis. The company has caused a more than fivefold increase in the price since 2008, with some customers paying more than $600 for two of these auto injection devices.

I used to take gobs of vitamins and supplements from Life Extension.org (LEF). I am sure they never hurt me, but I am not sure how much good they did me. I now take only a good multi vitamin, vitamin D3, and high quality fish oil pill.

I also may take a pill of cruciferous vegetable extracts because cruciferous vegetables are said to the world's most healthy (broccoli, Brussels sprouts, cabbage, cauliflower, collards, kale, turnips). I used to eat them after steaming them, but couldn't stand to eat them after a while. Now I just take the pills, which I purchase from LifeExtension.org.

Also, I may take Turmeric to avoid colds and other illnesses. Joshua Corn, the owner of "Stop Aging Now", says that Turmeric has just been found to help avoid early onset dementia as well. He says "By age 65, sadly 1 in 8 Americans will suffer from severe cognitive decline, and by age 80, an astonishing 1 in 2 will." Dementia has already claimed my good friend and my varsity debate team partner at the University of Georgia. I also have a keen interest in this because dementia has run heavily in my wife's family.

The Unbelievable Saga of William Faloon and LifeExtension.org

While most supplements are not needed, I should explain why we owe a debt of gratitude to William Faloon, the founder of LifeExtension.org. He will always be one of my heroes.

The Life Extension Foundation (LEF) was founded by Faloon and Saul Kent, a science journalist with an intense desire to find means of slowing aging — and ultimately of ending death. LEF studied scientific literature for evidence of life-extending properties of vitamins and other nutrients. The results of these researches were published in a magazine (currently LIFE EXTENSION) and made available as products through mail-order sales. Saul Kent has remained President, but Vice-President William Faloon has effectively acted as CEO after Saul began founding other new companies devoted to life-extension.

Shortly before opening-time on the morning of February 26, 1987 twenty-five armed Food and Drug Administration (FDA) agents & US marshals smashed through the glass doors of the Life Extension Foundation store, simultaneously raiding the nearby warehouse in Florida. With drawn guns, the agents lined LEF employees against the wall while seizing products, literature, documents, computers and personal effects — more than 80% of which were not within the authority of the search warrant.

Having lost most of their product inventory, LEF principals Saul Kent & Bill Faloon were facing 5-to-20 years in prison. All the attorneys they consulted recommended a guilty plea as the only possible means of reducing prison time. Instead, Kent & Faloon fought back both in the courts and through political action. A political coordinator's office was established at LEF. The LEF members wrote to their political leaders.

I remember that I was living in Alexandria, Va. then, and I frequently went to my local health food store. Every time I went in, I was asked to send a letter to my Congressman.

On January 9, 1991 the FDA raided the LEF Arizona Shipping Office with the complicity of the Arizona Board of Pharmacy. A permanent embargo was placed against all future shipments of 42 LEF products, including Life Extension Mix and Coenzyme-Q10. Fifteen days after the embargo, LEF lawyers handed a 300-page lawsuit to the Attorney General of Arizona — who promptly ordered the Pharmacy Board to lift the embargo. The Pharmacy Board Director agreed that his agents would take no future actions on behalf of the FDA without investigating matters themselves first.

The FDA then threatened that Kent & Faloon would become the target of criminal indictments that would "destroy their lives forever" and were told to plead guilty of crimes against the state. Kent & Faloon responded with a lawsuit against the FDA in a Florida District Court seeking an injunction against discriminatory prosecution.

On November 7, 1991 Kent & Faloon were arrested and thrown into an 8-by-8 Fort Lauderdale jail cubicle containing several men charged with drug-related crimes. Several hours later they were taken handcuffed before a magistrate who informed them that they were charged with 28 criminal counts, including conspiracy to sell unapproved drugs. After more hours in jail, they were released on $825,000 bail each.

Kent & Faloon retaliated by filing motions attacking the legal & constitutional foundation of the indictment. They charged that the FDA had illegally obtained the search warrant and had illegally seized many items not on the warrant.

Despite continued threats of more FDA indictments that could put Kent & Faloon in jail for the rest of their lives, LEF became the first company to offer pharmaceutical-grade Melatonin in the United States in 1992. In 1994, LEF established the "FDA Holocaust Museum" to document "the 70-year reign of terror that the FDA had perpetuated against Americans".

In 1995 the FDA began exerting strong pressure to bring its lengthy legal fight against the Life Extension Foundation to trial. The FDA told Kent & Faloon that in exchange for a guilty plea they would not have to go to prison and could continue doing business on a more limited basis. The FDA wanted to censor the contents of LIFE EXTENSION magazine and probably intended to "regulate" LEF by limiting the products they could sell. Instead of pleading guilty, Kent & Faloon filed a new battery of legal motions, escalated their political attacks on the FDA and began extensive preparations for their trial.

In November 1995, the FDA dropped all charges except the charge of "obstruction of justice" against Saul Kent. In February, 1996 even this charge was dropped. It was the first time in the history of the FDA that the agency had given-up on a criminal indictment against a political opponent.

I still may order a few supplements from LifeExtension.org, but I also order more of them from Amazon.com from such suppliers as Swanson and Tru Nature. They generally cost about half the prices of LifeExtension. org. Both Sam's Clubs and Costco have the best prices on large bottles of multiple vitamins as well as some special vitamins. For those who cannot swallow that many pills, they are available in a chewable form. Go to ConsumerLab.com if you have questions about quality of the supplements sold through these outlets.

At this point Life Extension has not taken a position one way or another on TA–65. Obviously, it would seriously damage their business if many more people started taking TA–65.

Turmeric is the best for avoiding colds and flu. It has been used for thousands of years in India for their curry spice food. They had no sanitation, and it kept them alive.

As one who gets on airplanes frequently, I have had bad experiences in breathing other people's stale air. Occasionally someone sitting near me would violently cough. Now I hardly ever get sick in those winter months. Recently, I recently cleaned out my cabinets and threw my expired cold medicine away.

Also, frequent trips on airplanes make you keenly aware how many obese people of both sexes and all ages there are in America. It is a shame that they are sentencing themselves to a shorter and sicker life.

Another good source of advice is Dr. Marc Micozzi. For a nominal fee, he will send you newsletters every week called Dr. Micozzi's Insider's Cures. Like William Faloon before him, he is a crusader against "Big Pharma". He will also try to sell you his supplements.

I can't vouch for his supplements, but a couple of his recommendations are good. He was the first to challenge the $10 billion a year colonoscopy industry. This industry flourished after popular TV anchor Katie Couric's husband died of colon cancer. She even had the procedure done on television to dramatize the need for prevention. Since then doctors routinely prescribe them for their older patients. They are to be done every five years.

This is the most disgusting procedure I ever had done. I now take a simple stool sample, which is just as effective. Another thing he advises people to stop taking is lipid drugs. He sells supplements as well. However, I can't vouch for them. One is a tiny bottle that contains a liquid which contains three of the vitamins that I take.

The first definitive clinical human trials demonstrating that TA-65 lengthens chromosomes. Notably, this is the first double blind, placebo-controlled study to show actual lengthening of telomeres in humans.

The press release below provides the first scientific proof of the efficacy of TA-65

"NEW YORK, NY (PRWEB) JUNE 07, 2016
A new study, conducted on 97 relatively healthy cytomegalovirus-positive subjects a
TA-65® is a patented, all natural, plant-based compound
d that animal and in vitro studies have indicated activates telomerase, which may help maintain or rebuild parts of the chromosomes, called telomeres that diminish as people get older.
Telomeres protect the chromosome, preventing the loss of DNA to ensure cells replicate properly. As people age, telomeres shorten and leave the genetic DNA on the chromosomes vulnerable to damage and mutations. Over time, telomere shortening causes cells to die or to become senescent. By activating telomerase, an enzyme that adds nucleotides to telomeres, cells are able to live longer and continue to function properly.
This new study, published in Rejuvenation Research, confirms previous scientific studies demonstrating that TA-65MD® activates telomerase and lengthens telomeres in a statistically significant manner. Notably, this is the first double blind, placebo-controlled study to show actual lengthening of telomeres in humans.
"By activating telomerase, we can help slow and perhaps even reverse cellular aging. These findings are an exciting step in our goal to safely prolong the life of human cells," said Noel Thomas Patton, the founder of T.A. Sciences, "We have been a leader in telomerase research since 2002 and will continue to invest in valuable research to help further the field of telomere biology."
Study Summary:
Study participants: 97 men and women (53-87 years old)
Study length: 12 months
First study to show statistically significant ($p<0.005$) lengthening of telomeres in humans:
- Placebo Group – Decrease in median telomere length over 12 month
Median telomere length: ☐ 290 ± 100 bp
20th percentile telomere length: ☐ 170 ± 50 bp
- TA-65MD® Group – Increase vs placebo group in median telomere length over 12 months
Median telomere length: ☐ 533 ± 180 bp
20th percentile telomere length: ☐ 270 ± 90 bp

About T.A. Sciences®: Founded in 2002, T.A. Sciences® is the first healthcare company dedicated to creating research-based wellness products that help address cellular aging through Telomerase Activation. Built upon a foundation strongly grounded in scientific evidence, T.A. Sciences® is widely recognized as the leader in the field of Telomere Biology. TA-65MD® is available from licensed healthcare practitioners worldwide. For more information about T.A. Sciences®, visit http://www.tasciences.com."

The Price Drop after This Study

It was interesting to me that the price of TA 65 fell after this clinical study. TA Sciences had been holding the price at $600 per bottle for 90 pills, and the recommended dosage was four per day. The clinical study demonstrated that the optimum dosage was two per day. The price per bottle then fell to $428 per bottle on Amazon.com, which translates to $3,472 per year. It is affordable to people like me. However, I worry about the ordinary retiree who may not be able to afford it. This is especially true when you add the cost of a spouse; the annual cost would be $6,944. This is not reimbursed by health insurance, Medicare, or Medicaid although it would save all of these programs billions of dollars.

Subsequently, the price has bounced around, but I still get it through my doctor for about this price.

In fairness I will say that taking the TA 65 has enabled me to stop taking all prescription and nonprescription drugs except for Metformin and Jardiance, and I save a few hundred dollars monthly. I have cancelled my Medicare Advantage private insurance with Humana, and I rarefy go into a drug store any more. I only take Metformin and Jardiance to control my Type 2 diabetes. I estimate that the few natural supplements I take costs me about fifty cents a day. The only time I see a doctor is when I have my physical examination once a year.

Noel Thomas Patton, who is now 71, bought the patents from the GERON Corporation. His motivation was to be able to do all the things he enjoyed as a young man, such as dancing and skiing. He is quoted as saying that "I wanted to protect my own ass".

Regardless of anyone's motivations, I firmly believe that TA 65 will go down as the greatest medical breakthrough of the 21st Century.

The Harsh Overreach of the FTC

Unfortunately, the Federal Trade Commission (FTC) tried to halt the production and promotion of TA 65. In 2015, it sent a notice to TA Sciences and some smaller entities associated with them. The FTC demanded that they sign a consent order agreeing to halt their activities. When this letter was sent, there was no clinical evidence to prove the claims made by TA Sciences. However, when the clinical evidence became available, the FTC did not drop its legal action.

It is a supreme irony that the Federal Trade Commission was trying to put the company that is selling TA 65 out of business. It is also ironic because the modern FTC was in large part the creation of consumer activist Mike Pertchuk.

The FTC should be encouraging the spending of a small fraction of the billions of dollars currently spent on our broken health care system to promote and subsidize TA 65. Other countries such as China, where the Astragalus plant is grown, certainly will.

I travelled to China at the end of 2016 as the guest of a billionaire known as Chairman Shi. He has built the largest Marriott Hotel in the word and plans to have a world anti-aging conference. I gave him a copy of Dr. Michael Fossel's latest book and a bottle of TA 65.

MY ROLE in TA 65 as a LAWYER

Dr. Ed Park of Newport Beach, California is responsible for my introduction to TA 65. While he had nothing to do with inventing it, he was one of the first people to try it out on himself. In addition, he was the first doctor to widely popularize it. He got into trouble when Noel Thomas Patten and he were interviewed by Suzanne Somers, a beautiful 69 year old actress and former Playboy Magazine cover girl. Patton is a wealthy businessman who had purchased the patents for TA 65 from the Geron Corporation.

Based on this interview, the Federal Trade Commission, The Federal Trade commission went after both Patton and Park. They were insisting that Patton and Park sign a consent order to cease selling and promoting TA 65. They intended to enforce this order in the Southern Judicial District of New York because that is where Patton is located.

No two defendants could have been less alike. Patton is rich and Park is far from rich. He had to use crowd funding to pay my modest monthly fee of $2,000 per month.

However, it was obvious the FTC was making a serious case out of this. When I would get on the phone with them there was always a team of five lawyers on the other end of the line. I had only one young trial lawyer in my office.

In an act of desperation, I turned to an old friend who I helped to secure the job of the Chairman of the Federal Trade Commission under President Jimmy Carter. As a native of Georgia I had worked in the campaign of Jimmy Carter. Mike Pertchuk asked for my support in his quest to be appointed as the Chairman of the FTC. I knew him as a fellow Senate Staff Director, so I gave him my support. He got the job and then created the modern Federal Trade Commission. I had lost contact with Mike, but I tracked him down. He is now in his early 80's and still a consumer activist.

I asked for Mike's help and he did not promise to do anything. However, things suddenly changed. The FTC suddenly called to say they were dropping the case. I tried to thank Mike but he never admitted he did anything.

RUSSIA IS ACTIVE IN AGE MANAGEMENT

Another country active in age management is Russia. Dr. Aubrey de Grey of England is an adjunct professor at the University of Moscow. As Dr. Fossel relates in his latest book, Russian scientists have long been interested in curing aging. I expect Vladimir Putin to live a longer than former President Obama—--that is unless Obama begins taking TA 65 during his retirement years. Certainly he already has a flat belly.

I have recently begun using a product produced by Bill Andrews who operates a lab called Sierra Sciences. It developed a product called Product B. He was one of the scientists who were involved in discovering the molecule that would come to be known as TA 65, while he and Calvin Harley were working for the GERON Corporation. I have gotten to know him because he is a fellow graduate of the University of Georgia.

His motto is "Cure aging or die trying". Moreover, Sierra Sciences is continuing efforts to perfect the telomerase activator by doing thousands of tests in his labs at Sierra Sciences.

I have told Bill that he has to be crazy to compete in his annual ultra-marathon races in Death Valley. However, he laughs me off and says he thrives on those temperatures of up to 130 degrees Fahrenheit

I have tried another product on the market called Crackaging CA-100. It is 100% Natural Super-Absorption Cycloastragenol. It also is made from the root of the astragalus plant, which contains the molecule that TA 65 comes from and is grown in China. Like TA 65, it is available on Amazon.com, but at a very modest price. I tried it myself but it ran my blood sugar numbers up, so I quit. However, I had supplied it to my older brother, who does not have Type 2 diabetes like me. He reports good results. Also I give it to my aging German shepherd dog. Both products are available on Amazon.com, so you can try both,

I hope that someday a rich philanthropist will buy the relevant patents from Patton and make what is known as TA 65 available to people of all income levels. Obviously, there are a number of rich tycoons who could afford to do so.

How Long Can We Expect to Live Strong, Fit, and Sexy?

In 2007 a retired lawyer named Chris Crowley coauthored a book about this topic, "Younger Next Year: Live Strong, Fit, and Sexy-Until you're 80 and beyond". His coauthor was Dr. Harry S. Lodge, a noted gerontologist. Lodge's part of the book contains some helpful insights on how our body's age. I thought so highly of it that I gave it to an old client of mine.

Crowley favored a daily workout on a spinning machine, as well as strength training twice a week. Also, a young lady who worked for me taught a class in spinning at a nearby class in Washington, DC. She successfully did so to lose weight. When I last checked on Crowley, he had fulfilled at least part of his goals and seemed to be going strong at age 81. Unfortunately, his coauthor Dr. Lodge recently died of prostate cancer.

Crowley maintains a website www.youngernextyear.com he invites people to hire him as a motivational speaker. I hope that Crowley reads this book when it is published. He may wish to revise his book and substitute the number 100 for the number 80.

The Tipping Point

Until I was completing this book, I did not realize that we had come so far so fast. Indeed, we have reached a tipping point in human history. We appear to at last found "the fountain of youth" Ponce de Leon searched for in Florida in the 16th century. However, continued progress will not come easy.

Entire industries could be decimated. Most of the people in the health care industry are good people devoted to caring for their patients. It has long been thought that doctors and nurses are part of a noble profession. I agree that this is noble industry, but when people's livelihoods are threatened, they fight back fiercely.

In my case, I was fortunate enough to have a doctor, Dr. Lucian Rice, who had been an active member of the American Academy of Anti-Aging Medicine. When Dr. Park made me aware of TA 65, Rice had just attended one of their conventions. Representatives of TA Sciences made a presentation at the convention. Thus, he did not have the negative reaction that most doctors do. He was happy to monitor my health as I took the capsules.

Unfortunately, the response of many family doctors is that it is not safe and it causes cancer. There is absolutely no scientific evidence of this. The problem with cancer cells is that they are already immortal. The only other kind of immortal body cell is the embryonic stem cell.

Moreover, Maria Blasco, a prolific scientist who heads the Telomeres and Telomerase Group at the Spanish National Cancer Research Centre reported that in a 2015 study of genetically engineered mice; TA-65 rescued cells in jeopardy and improved health without increasing cancer incidence, which is a risk when cells can divide for longer periods of time.

While the huge pharmaceutical industry is primarily interested in maximizing the profits for their shareholders as well as increasing the huge salaries of their chief executives, they too consider themselves indispensable to mankind.

They have to spend a huge amount of money to get through the tests that are required by the FDA. People who follow the stock markets know that drug company stocks rise and fall on news of whether a new drug has been approved by FDA. Then they only have to protect themselves against lawsuits by lawyers in the class action lawsuit industry.

A scandal that broke as my last book book was going to press is illustrative. The Mylan drug company had manufactured a little device called the EpiPen Pen for years. Then Mylan" one competitor stopped making the device. There was suddenly a 400% increase in the price of these life saving devices. They are essential to people who tend to suffer from anaphylaxis.

There have been howls of outrage from Congress. Senator Klobuchar of Minnesota was particularly outraged, as her daughter relies on EpiPen. Congressional hearings have were held on this subject.

In the meantime, our oldest consumer activist, Ralph Nader, has returned and was interviewed on national TV. The 82 year old Nader seems as alert and articulate as ever. He was responsible for the passage of several laws and the founding of the Federal Trade Commission (FTC).

The Mylan CEO Heather Bresch says that American should redirect their anger toward a "broken health care system". She has pointed to the lack of transparency in the complex health care system—with bigger payments for everyone from the pharmacy to the wholesaler. She says this incentivizes higher prices in the industry.

Even more ominous are her comments comparing the health care crisis to the real estate mortgage crisis of 2008. She said "Our health care system is in crisis…this bubble is going to burst",

The operators of nursing homes are indispensable in caring for our aged parents. It is generally a poorly paid but important job. Both my mother and my mother in law went through this, but their quality of life for the last ten years was terrible.

To make matters even worse, some trial lawyers have television ads offering to sue nursing homes "if your loved ones are not being properly taken care of".

All of these groups have powerful lobbies. As reported earlier in this book, the FDA tried to wipe out the supplement industry in the 1990's. Now that this industry has credibility, the FTC used the full force of its authority to wipe out TA 65. However, I am confident that when the truth is out it cannot squelched. In the words of Victor Hugo, "No force on earth can stop an idea whose time has come".

A Modest Proposal

As this book goes to print, there has been some press on the 50th anniversary of the Age Discrimination Act of 1967. As someone who recently was egregiously harmed by age discrimination, I have a personal interest in this. The expert in this field of law is Patricia G. Barnes, the author of "Betrayed: The Legalization of Age Discrimination in the Workplace".

I have been trying to get AARP, Inc. , which was formerly the American Association of Retired Persons, to take up this cause, but have been unable to get their attention. I welcome your support in this area.

Many economic commentators have pointed out the rise of contract workers who have very little protection in the workface. In an April 20, 2015 report, the U. S. Government Accountability Office pointed out that increasing millions of workers do not have the traditional employee protections and benefits. The report citation is GAO-15-168R Contingent Workforce.

This means that more and more aging workers can be discriminated against and have few legal protections. They are contract or "at will" employees. They are forced to retire long before they are ready, and they do not have even the meager protections that are currently available under the Age Discrimination Act of 1967. There have been some huge verdicts awarded recently, but not for contract workers. This will be the subject of an upcoming book by me.

26407375R00022

Printed in Great Britain
by Amazon